SOLO VIOLIN

Wolfgang Amadeus MOZART

SINFONIA CONCERTANTE

in

E-FLAT MAJOR

for

VIOLIN, VIOLA *and* ORCHESTRA

KV364

ADAGIO *in* E MAJOR

KV261

RONDO *in* C MAJOR

KV373

for VIOLIN *and* ORCHESTRA

To access audio visit:
www.halleonard.com/mylibrary

Enter Code
3371-5024-5663-0114

ISBN: 978-1-59615-780-4

Music Minus One

EXCLUSIVELY DISTRIBUTED BY

HAL•LEONARD®

Visit Hal Leonard Online at
www.halleonard.com

Contact Us:
Hal Leonard
7777 West Bluemound Road
Milwaukee, WI 53213
Email: info@halleonard.com

In Europe contact:
Hal Leonard Europe Limited
Distribution Centre, Newmarket Road
Bury St Edmunds, Suffolk, IP33 3YB
Email: info@halleonardeurope.com

In Australia contact:
Hal Leonard Australia Pty. Ltd.
4 Lentara Court
Cheltenham, Victoria, 3192 Australia
Email: info@halleonard.com.au

Mozart and His Sinfonia Concertante

Wolfgang Amadeus Mozart
(1756-1791)

It was during a European tour in 1777 that Wolfgang Amadeus Mozart began to explore the genre of the sinfonia concertante, which lies between concerto and symphony, for a future work. This culminated in 1779 with the completion of his *Sinfonia Concertante for Violin, Viola & Orchestra*.

It was in France that the extremely talented George Boulogne, Chevalier de Saint-George (1745-1799) promoted and further developed this form of composition (successor to the Baroque concerto grosso form) during the classical era, in which soloists played a clear and virtuosic role, but were also firmly integrated into the fabric of a symphony-like work and participated in the entire work, not only in the solo sections. George Boulogne was a bold and adventuresome African-French composer, conductor, musician, fencer, equestrian and military colonel during the French Revolution.

Though many have held that Saint-George's fame has been diminished due to bigotry regarding his mixed-race parentage, Mozart cannot have been oblivious to his presence and his advances in the French (and European) world of music. His choice of the form may also stand testament to his exposure to Saint-George's works in this format.

Cast in a typical three-movement form, Mozart scored in addition to the solo violin and viola, two oboes, two horns and a string section. Throughout all the movements, the two lead instruments share a well-balanced sense of importance and their "dialogue" is quite playful and well-defined. Mozart's use of complex dynamics in the orchestra shows the progress made in symphonic performance standards during the mid-to-late 1700s.

Many may notice a familiar strain when listening to the second movement: this could be because the first two phrases were adapted for use in the 1968 motion picture, *The Thomas Crown Affair*, where they were made familiar to generations of popular music-goers in the song "The Windmills of Your Mind."

We include on this album two other Mozart bon-bons for violin and orchestra: The *Rondo* in C major, KV373; and the *Adagio* in E major, KV261. Both complement in their smaller way the grandeur of the *Sinfonia Concertante*.

This MMO learning and performance edition gives you the opportunity to enjoy and study virtuoso Mario Hossen's performance; then consult his textual notes and stand front and center with the orchestra and perform them with the full orchestra! Enjoy!

Music Minus One

3170

CONTENTS

Sinfonia Concertante in E-Flat Major, KV364
   I.   *Allegro maestoso* 7
   II. *Andante* 14
   III. *Presto* 17

Adagio in E Major, KV261 24

Rondo in C Major, KV373 28

FOREWORD

 The **Sinfonia Concertante for Violin, Viola and Orchestra** in E-flat major, KV364 was written in 1779 during Mozart's tour in Europe that included Mannheim and Paris. In addition to the solo violin and viola, the accompanying orchestration of the work is for two oboes, two horns and strings. Mozart completed this "double concerto" in Salzburg in the summer of 1779, and very likely he was the soloist in its first performance. The composition's complex orchestral markings reflect the increasing technical demands of the European orchestra of that era, and this particular development was certainly strongly influenced by Mozart's visit to the Mannheim orchestra 1777–1779. Mozart might have viewed the *Sinfonia Concertante* as a challenge to make this new genre popular in Salzburg, especially since here the corresponding good instrumentalists were available.

Mozart's shorter concerted works for violin and orchestra were largely composed in Salzburg between 1773 and 1776. It is not kown whether they were written for himself (as he was a fine violinist), or rather for a member of the Salzburg court orchestra. Probably they were composed for the Italian violinist Antonio Brunetti, the concertmaster of the Salzburg orchestra. Brunetti is known to have performed them after taking the position, and the present "Adagio" is almost certainly that referred to by Leopold Mozart in a letter to his son as "the 'Adagio' you wrote specially for Brunetti." An indication that Mozart wrote the works for himself might be the fact that he composed some sections anew at the request of his colleague. For the A major concerto, KV219, Mozart in 1776 composed this second "Adagio" (KV261) because the original appeared "too artificial" to Brunetti. The serenity of the movement is enhanced by its orchestral accompaniment, scored for muted strings, with two horns and two flutes replacing the oboes. Mozart composed the "Rondo" for violin and orchestra, KV 373, for Brunetti as well. The orchestration of the work is: two oboes, two horns and strings. The first public performance was on 8 April 1779 in Vienna.

IMPORTANT NOTES

ARTICULATION

Basically, the performer must learn how to express the character of the piece, and how to deliver each passage according to its required and particular taste, to know exactly how to perform all the various bowing arts, dynamics in the proper place and degree.

The famous flute player and composer J. Quantz (1697–1773) described in his famous theoretical book *Versuch einer Anweisung die Floete traversiere zu spielen* (1752), the choice of appropriate articulation as a process of giving "life" to the notes. The performer should add the life (character, spirit) to the music through the proper phrasing, bow-stroke, and fingering for each note. The bow-stroke provides the means for artistically achieving articulation, and for varying a single idea in diverse ways. The performer must enter into the passion and message of the musical work. Regarding Mozart's interpretation and the proper manner of bowing, the recommended source absolutely is his father Leopold Mozart (1719–1787). Leopold, an excellent violinist and respectable composer, wrote in 1756 his best known work, a method for the violin entitled *Versuch einer gruendlichen Violinshule*, perhaps one of the most solid books of its kind and a main source for the study of Wolfgang Amadeus Mozart.

Regarding the articulation and bow-strokes, Leopold Mozart devotes considerable space. Some examples:

"The player must be guided by passion. Sometimes a note requires a rather vigorous attack, at other times a moderate one, at still other times one that is barely perceptible. The first usually occurs in connection with a sudden expression that all the instruments make together; as rule is indicated by the direction fp... The accent, expression, or intensity of the tone will fall, as a rule, on the strong or initial note that the Italians call the nota buona..."

"...the bowing gives life to the notes; it produces now a modest, now an impertinent, now a serious or playful tone; now coaxing, or grave and sublime; now a sad or merry melody; and is therefore the medium by the reasonable use of which we are able to rouse in the hearers the aforesaid affects..."

The usual and normal bow-stroke in the 18th century was a *non-legato* stroke. Depending on its length, tempo, and musical context, various nuances were applied.

BOWING AND BOW-STROKES

"Marry and playful passages must be played with light, short, and lifted bow, happily and rapidly; just as in slow, sad pieces one performs them with long strokes of the bow, simply and tenderly."
—*J. Quantz*

During the classical period, the down-bow must normally be used for the first of each measure. The rule was also applied to accented parts of single beats when the tempo permitted and, as a logical complement, the up-bow was used on unaccented notes and unaccented parts of beats. Of course, in practical life we have many modifications and exceptions, depending on a fast or slow tempo, and the manner of character and expression.

"Except when the measure begins with a rest, the first note of every measure is played down-bow, even if two down-bows come together…"
—*Leopold Mozart*

The individual bow-strokes include a normal *non legato* stroke and a *staccato* stroke. According to Quantz, the *staccato* stroke over a note meant a lifted bow, and the *staccato* dot (.) meant that a detached bow-stroke remained on the string. A lifted bow is involved in playing certain dotted figures. The dotted note is elongated as a rule, and the following short note is often written with a *staccato* stroke and must be played with lifted bow.

Especially in the slow movement *"Legato"* introduced in the classical period the realization of the ideal of a smooth, round, continuous and beautiful tone.

"…*legato* bow-stroke, which is the melody-producing stroke, will continue to be one of the strokes most used, the stroke of them all which every violinist must develop in a really perfect manner if his string-song is to be unbroken and his tone production equalized and connected… Do not raise the finger on one string before the tone of the next string sounds!"
—*Leopold Auer*

THE STACCATO

In the 18th century, the term *staccato* indicated a separation between notes. The general effect is a detaching or noticeable degree of articulation. *Staccato* applied to notes normally results in dividing the written note half into sound and half into rest, with some feeling of accent. The manner of performing *staccato* differs at different tempi. In *adagio*, the *staccato* is not as short as in *allegro*, otherwise the *adagio* would sound too dry and thin. Regarding the articulation in a slow tempo, individual notes marked *staccato* must be performed with lifted bow, at faster tempi the bow remaining on the string. If dots (*puncte*) stand over notes, they must be played pushed (*gestossen*) but not lifted.

Regarding the slurred *staccato*, Leopold Mozart is consistent in directing that slurred staccato with strokes must be played with a "lifted" bow. The dots under a slur are separated from each other by a slight pressure of the bow, so all notes within the slur must be separated from each other. The general effect of the 18th century *staccato* is a detaching or notable degree of articulation.

THE APPOGGIATURAS

Modern musicians often wonder why *appoggiaturas* were written as "small" notes… There are several reasons for this form of notation. First, to show the function of the note as an *appoggiatura* (an accented and frequently dissonant note), second to prevent further ornamentation, and the last reason is that small notes sometimes implied a dynamic interpretation different from the usual "big note" notation.

THE CADENZA (caprice, fantasia)

The *cadenzas* generally ended with trill on the dominant, leading effectively to the return of the orchestra on the tonic. J. Quantz writes, explaining the spirit and intent of the cadenza so: "The greatest beauty lies in that, as something unexpected, they should astonish the listener in a fresh and striking manner and, at the same time, impel to the highest pitch the agitation of passion which is sought after…"

FINGERING, VIBRATO

The use of open string is increasingly restricted, especially in melodies, so we can escape the difference in tone or *timbre* between open and stopped strings. Regarding the change of position, Leopold Mozart gives three reasons for the use of position playing: necessity, convenience and elegance. The higher positions are used to keep the elegant units of tone color on a single string rather than the contrast of several in the lower positions.

In modern violin playing, *vibrato* is considered as part of sound production. During the 18th century, *vibrato* was used as an ornament to be applied occasionally and for specific tone expressions. So after ca. 1750, continuous *vibrato* appears as a part of the left-hand technique. According to G. Tartini and L. Mozart, the *vibrato* could be slow, increasing, or rapid in oscillation.

THE ORCHESTRA

"…all the ensemble players must observe each other carefully, and especially watch the leader; not only so that they begin well together but that they may play steadily in the same tempo and with the same expression."

—*Leopold Mozart*

J. Quantz specifies the number of string players in the orchestra. When one uses four violins (two each for violin I and violin II), there should be one viola, one cello, and one medium-sized double bass. For twelve violins, three violas are needed plus four cellos and one or two basses.

RHYTHM, TEMPO, KEYS

"Time is the Soul of Music"
 —*Leopold Mozart, Versuch einer gruendlichen Violinshule (1756)*

"Time is the measure of movement and pulsation"… "Rhythm is an aggregation of time arranged according to certain rules."
—*Aristide Quintillian*

"The laws of beauty demand that the time occupied by the performance of a musical work be divided in such a manner that the feeling of the auditor is able to discern, without effort, a regularity in the various groups of sounds and of words, as well as in the periodical return of pulsation. Such an order is nothing less than rhythm, the manifestation of the principle of unity, of symmetry, applied to the arts of movement."
—*Francois-Auguste Gaevert*

As we know, the earliest method of measuring tempo was human pulse. Although the metronome is certainly a useful tool (Johann Maeltzel manufactured the metronome), tempo is affected by many factors, such as the acoustic of the hall, the particular instruments being used, and any personal feeling at the moment of performance. Very often, the tempo indicates not the speed, but much more the mood, character and spirit of expressions in the music. Leopold Mozart places great attention on tempo: "Every melodious piece has at least one phrase from which one can recognize quite surely what sort of speed the piece demands." Jean-Philippe Rameau makes a similar comment: "When one has mastered a piece, one grasps its sense unconsciously, and soon one feels its right tempo."

The view of Mozart and Rameau is somewhat optimistic as regards the modern musician. The varying resonance of halls and many other musical factors enforce a certain flexibility in this matter if one is to achieve the best musical effect.

For example:
"Adagio," KV261: you must have a singing and expressive character, belonging to the cantabile type, and performed not too slowly. We recommend not to add any ornamentation into a piece that is already beautiful and therefore un-improvable.

Leopold Mozart comments about those who think they must "befrill" an *adagio cantabile* and "make out of one note at least a dozen. Such note-murderers expose thereby their bad judgment to the light, and tremble when they have to sustain a long note or perform only a few notes stingingly, without inserting their usual preposterous and laughable frippery."

Regarding the character of the keys; we should not forget that during the classical and baroque period, consideration of the key characteristics did influence both composers and performers in many cases, and the key was one of many features that contributed to the spirit of the work.

Sinfonia Concertante, KV364 in E-Flat Major-
E-flat major: "pathetic; concerned with serious and plaintive things; bitterly hostile to all lasciviousness"
—*Johann Matheson (1713)*

"Adagio" KV261 in E Major-
E Major: "…expresses a desperate or wholly fatal sadness incomparably well; most suited for extremes of helpless and hopeless love"
—*Johann Matheson (1713)*

"Rondo" KV373 in C Major-
C Major: "rude and impudent character; suited to rejoicing"
—*Johann Matheson (1713)*

"songs of mirth and rejoicing"
—*Jean-Philippe Rameau (Paris, 1722)*

SINFONIA CONCERTANTE

for Violin, Viola and Orchestra
E-flat major ♀ Es-dur
KV364

Edited by Mario Hossen

Wolfgang Amadeus Mozart
1756-1791

Allegro maestoso
TUTTI

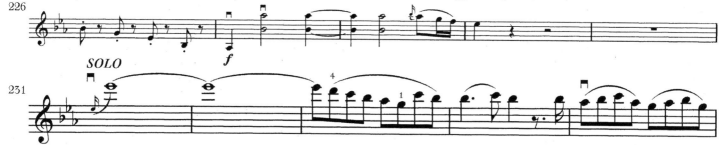

306

309

312

316

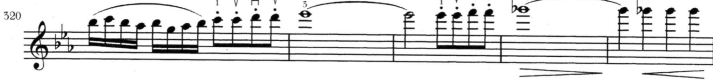

320

325

330

335

Cadenza

(1)

(4)

Andante

Cadenza

Presto

154

160

168

173

179

185

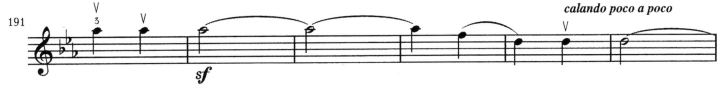

191

197

203

209

215

Wolfgang Amadeus
MOZART

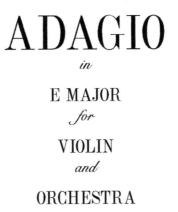

ADAGIO

in

E MAJOR

for

VIOLIN

and

ORCHESTRA

KV261

ADAGIO

for Violin and Orchestra
E major ♀ E-dur
KV261

Wolfgang Amadeus Mozart
1756-1791

Edited by Mario Hossen

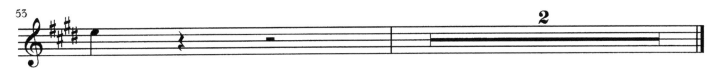

Wolfgang Amadeus

MOZART

RONDO

in

C MAJOR

for

VIOLIN

and

ORCHESTRA

KV373

MMO 3170

RONDO

for Violin and Orchestra
C major 𝄞 C-dur
KV373

Edited by Mario Hossen

Wolfgang Amadeus Mozart
1756-1791

Allegretto grazioso

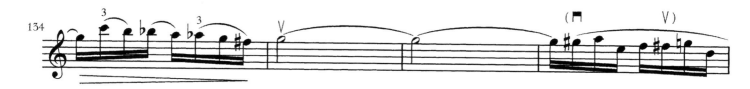

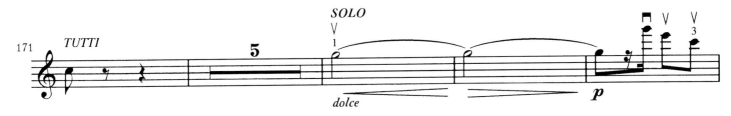

1020
337